KINGFISHER BOOKS
Grisewood & Dempsey Inc.
95 Madison Avenue
New York, New York 10016

First American edition 1993
2 4 6 8 10 9 7 5 3 1

Library of Congress Cataloging-in-Publication Data
The Little book of poems / selected by Caroline Walsh : illustrated by
Gilly Marklew. — 1st American ed.
p. cm.
Summary: A collection of famous and lesser known poems by such
authors as Robert Louis Stevenson, Kenneth Grahame, X. J. Kennedy,
and Christina Rossetti.
1. Children's poetry, English. 2. Children's poetry, American.
[1. American poetry — Collections. 2. English poetry — Collections.]
I. Walsh, Caroline. II. Marklew, Gilly, ill.
PR1175.3.L57 1993
821.008'09282 — dc20 92-29126 CIP AC

ISBN 1-85697-887-7

Printed in Hong Kong

THE LITTLE BOOK OF

POEMS

Selected by Caroline Walsh • Illustrated by Gilly Marklew

Kingfisher Books

NEW YORK

Contents

Contents

Monday's child is fair of face,
Tuesday's child is full of grace,
Wednesday's child is full of woe,
Thursday's child has far to go,
Friday's child is loving and giving,
Saturday's child works hard for a living,
And the child that is born on the Sabbath day
Is bonny and blithe, and good and gay.

TRADITIONAL

Six Weeks Old

He is so small, he does not know
The summer sun, the winter snow;
The spring that ebbs and comes again,
All this is far beyond his ken.

A little world he feels and sees:
His mother's arms, his mother's knees;
He hides his face against her breast,
And does not care to learn the rest.

CHRISTOPHER MORLEY

Chamber Music

Lean out of the window,
  Golden hair,
I hear you singing
  A merry air.

My book is closed;
  I read no more,
Watching the fire dance
  On the floor.

I have left my books:
  I have left my room:
For I heard you singing
  Through the gloom.

Singing and singing
  A merry air.
Lean out of the window
  Golden hair.

JAMES JOYCE

Grandpa

Grandpa's hands are as rough as garden sacks
And as warm as pockets.
His skin is crushed paper round his eyes
Wrapping up their secrets.

BERLIE DOHERTY

Bread and Cherries

"Cherries, ripe Cherries!"
    The old woman cried,
In her snowy white apron,
    And basket beside;
And the little boys came,
    Eyes shining, cheeks red,
To buy bags of cherries,
    To eat with their bread.

WALTER DE LA MARE

"Loveliest of trees, the cherry now"

Loveliest of trees, the cherry now
Is hung with bloom along the bough,
And stands about the woodland ride
Wearing white for Eastertide.

Now, of my threescore years and ten,
Twenty will not come again,
And take from seventy springs a score,
It only leaves me fifty more.

And since to look at things in bloom
Fifty springs are little room,
About the woodlands I will go
To see the cherry hung with snow.

A.E. HOUSMAN

19

This Is Just to Say

I have eaten
the plums
that were in
the icebox

and which
you were probably
saving
for breakfast

Forgive me
they were delicious
so sweet
and so cold.

WILLIAM CARLOS WILLIAMS

Mice

I think mice
Are rather nice.

Their tails are long,
Their faces small,
They haven't any
Chins at all.

Their ears are pink,
Their teeth are white,
They run about
The house at night.

They nibble things
They shouldn't touch
And no one seems
To like them much.

But *I* think mice
Are nice.

ROSE FYLEMAN

23

The Cat of Cats

I am the cat of cats. I am
    The everlasting cat!
Cunning, and old, and sleek as jam,
    The everlasting cat!
I hunt the vermin in the night —
    The everlasting cat!
For I see best without the light —
    The everlasting cat!

WILLIAM BRIGHTY RANDS

Seven Blackbirds

Seven blackbirds in a tree,
Count them and see what they be.
One for sorrow
Two for joy
Three for a girl
Four for a boy;
Five for silver
Six for gold
Seven for a secret
That's never been told.

TRADITIONAL

Ducks' Ditty

All along the backwater,
Through the rushes tall,
Ducks are a-dabbling.
Up tails all!

Ducks' tails, drakes' tails,
Yellow feet a-quiver,
Yellow bills all out of sight
Busy in the river!

Slushy green undergrowth
Where the roach swim —
Here we keep our larder,
Cool and full and dim.

Every one for what he likes!
We like to be
Head down, tails up,
Dabbling free!

High in the blue above
Swifts whirl and call —
We are down a-dabbling
Up tails all!

KENNETH GRAHAME

Bee

You want to make some honey?
All right. Here's the recipe.
Pour the juice of a thousand flowers
Through the sweet tooth of a Bee.

X.J. KENNEDY

Seaweed

Seaweed sways and sways and swirls
as if swaying were its form of stillness;
and if it flushes against fierce rock
it slips over it as shadows do, without hurting itself.

D.H. LAWRENCE

Ariel's Song

Full fathom five thy father lies;
  Of his bones are coral made;
Those are pearls that were his eyes:
  Nothing of him that doth fade,
But doth suffer a sea-change
Into something rich and strange.
Sea-nymphs hourly ring his knell:
                              Ding-dong.
Hark now I hear them, ding-dong bell.

WILLIAM SHAKESPEARE

The Whale

— Warm and buoyant in his oily mail
Gambols on seas of ice the unwieldy whale,
Wide waving fins round floating islands urge
His bulk gigantic through the troubled surge.

O'er the white wave he lifts his nostril bare,
And spouts transparent columns into air;
The silvery arches catch the setting beams,
And transient rainbows tremble o'er the streams.

ERASMUS DARWIN

Unicorn

The Unicorn with the long white horn
   Is beautiful and wild.
He gallops across the forest green
So quickly that he's seldom seen
Where Peacocks their blue feathers preen
   And strawberries grow wild.
He flees the hunter and the hounds,
Upon black earth his white hoof pounds,
Over cold mountain streams he bounds
   And comes to a meadow mild;
There, when he kneels to take his nap,
He lays his head in a lady's lap
   As gently as a child.

WILLIAM JAY SMITH

Ah! Sunflower

Ah, Sunflower! weary of time,
Who countest the steps of the Sun,
Seeking after that sweet golden clime
Where the traveller's journey is done:

Where the Youth pined away with desire,
And the pale Virgin shrouded in snow
Arise from their graves, and aspire
Where my Sunflower wishes to go.

WILLIAM BLAKE

Happy Thought

The world is so full of a number of things,
I'm sure we should all be as happy as kings.

ROBERT LOUIS STEVENSON

43

44

Dandelions

Over the climbing meadows
Where the swallow shadows float,
These are the small gold buttons
On earth's green, windy coat.

FRANCES FROST

Clouds

White sheep, white sheep,
On a blue hill,
When the wind stops
You all stand still.
When the wind blows
You walk away slow.
White sheep, white sheep,
Where do you go?

CHRISTINA ROSSETTI

The Rainbow

Even the rainbow has a body
made of the drizzling rain
and is an architecture of glistening atoms
built up, built up.
Yet you can't lay your hand on it
nay, nor even your mind.

D.H. LAWRENCE

"Blazing in Gold"

Blazing in Gold and quenching in Purple
Leaping like Leopards to the Sky
Then at the feet of the old Horizon
Laying her spotted Face to die
Stooping as low as the Otter's Window
Touching the Roof and tinting the Barn
Kissing her Bonnet to the Meadow
And the Juggler of Day is gone

EMILY DICKINSON

"O Thought I!"

O thought I!
What a beautiful thing
God has made winter to be
by stripping the trees
and letting us see
their shapes and forms.
What a freedom does it seem
to give to the storms.

DOROTHY WORDSWORTH

Watching You Skating

I see two skates
Blue sliding into silver
Silver gliding into blue

I see two moons
One moon reflected in each of the skates
Carrying you

You zip across the blue and silver pond
I am wonderfully fond
Of the moon and the moon-faced pond and you

ADRIAN MITCHELL

The Horseman

I heard a horseman
  Ride over the hill;
The moon shone clear,
The night was still;
His helm was silver,
  And pale was he;
And the horse he rode
  Was of ivory.

WALTER DE LA MARE

The Night Will Never Stay

The night will never stay,
The night will still go by,
Though with a million stars
You pin it to the sky;

Though you bind it with the blowing wind
And buckle it with the moon,
The night will slip away
Like sorrow or a tune.

ELEANOR FARJEON

Index of Authors and First Lines

Acknowledgments

For permission to reproduce copyright material, acknowledgment and thanks are due to the following:

Berlie Doherty for "Grandpa" from *Another First Poetry Book* ed. John Foster; Houghton Mifflin Company for "Dandelions" by Frances Frost from *Pool in the Meadow*; Doubleday, a division of Bantam Doubleday Dell Publishing Group for "Mice" by Rose Fyleman, copyright 1931, 1932 by Doubleday; Curtis Brown Ltd. for "Bee" by X.J. Kennedy from *Did Adam Name the Vinagaroon?*, copyright © 1982 by X.J. Kennedy; The Peters Fraser and Dunlop Group Ltd. for "Watching You Skating" by Adrian Mitchell from *Nothingmas Day*, copyright © 1984 by Adrian Mitchell. None of Adrian Mitchell's poems are to be used in connection with any examination whatsoever; Harper & Row Publishers Inc. for "Six Weeks Old" from *Chimneysmoke* by Christopher Morley (Lippincott), copyright © 1921, 1949 by Christopher Morley; William Jay Smith for "Unicorn" from *Laughing Time: Nonsense Poems* by William Jay Smith, copyright © 1953, 1955, 1957, 1959, 1968, 1974, 1980 by William Jay Smith. Reprinted by permission of Farrar, Straus & Giroux Inc.

Every effort has been made to obtain permission from copyright holders. If, regrettably, any omissions have been made, we shall be pleased to make suitable corrections in any reprint.